ISBN 978-0-364-56123-2
PIBN 11276031

1 MONTH OF
FREE
READING

at
www.ForgottenBooks.com

By purchasing this book you are eligible for one month membership to ForgottenBooks.com, giving you unlimited access to our entire collection of over 1,000,000 titles via our web site and mobile apps.

To claim your free month visit:
www.forgottenbooks.com/free1276031

English
Français
Deutsche
Italiano
Español
Português

www.forgottenbooks.com

Mythology Photography **Fiction**
Fishing Christianity **Art** Cooking
Essays Buddhism Freemasonry
Medicine **Biology** Music **Ancient
Egypt** Evolution Carpentry Physics
Dance Geology **Mathematics** Fitness
Shakespeare **Folklore** Yoga Marketing
Confidence Immortality Biographies
Poetry **Psychology** Witchcraft
Electronics Chemistry History **Law**
Accounting **Philosophy** Anthropology
Alchemy Drama Quantum Mechanics
Atheism Sexual Health **Ancient History**
Entrepreneurship Languages Sport
Paleontology Needlework Islam
Metaphysics Investment Archaeology
Parenting Statistics Criminology
Motivational

INDEX OF ORGANISMS AND NON-PARASITIC DISEASES

in

THE PLANT DISEASE REPORTER

SUPPLEMENTS 121 - 128

Prepared by Nellie W. Nance

Plant Disease Reporter
Supplement ·129

December 31, 1940

Parris, G. K. A check list of fungi, bacteria, nematodes and viruses occurring in Hawaii, and their hosts, Supplement 121:1-91.

Darker, G. D. A brief host index of some plant pathogens and virus diseases in eastern Asia. Supplement 122:93-123.

Cooke, Wm. Bridge. Preliminary host index to fungi of Mount Shasta, California. Supplement 123:125-133.

Barss, Howard P. Proceedings of the third National Plant Nematode Conference. Supplement 124:135-150.

Maneval, W. E. Some recent records of plant pathogens in Missouri. Supplement 125:151-164. (These are listed alphabetically).

Melchers, L. E. and Alvin E. Lowe. The reaction of sorghum varieties and hybrids to milo disease. Supplement 126:165-175.

Edson, H. A., and Jessie I. Wood. Crop losses from plant diseases in the United States in 1939. Supplement 127:177-209.

Nance, Nellie W. Diseases of plants in the United States in 1939. Supplement 128:210-378.

A

Actinomyces sp., sweetpotato, 189, 271.
    scabies, garden beet, 253.
        potato, 191, 287.
Adelopus balsamicola, Abies lasio-
        carpa, 346.
Albinism, Brassica oleracea var.
        broccoli, 255.
    peanut, 325.

Albinism, pepper, 261.
Albugo bliti, Amaranthus retroflexus,
        350.
    candida, Capsella bursa-pastoris,
        355.
        horseradish, 285.
        radish, 285.
    ipomoeae-panduranae, Ipomoea
            hederacea, 363.

Albugo ipomoeae-panduranae, Ipomoea
      pandurata, 364.
    sweetpotato, 271.
  occidentalis, spinach, 293.
  platensis, Boerhavia erecta, 353.
  tragopogonis, salsify, 294.
Alkali soil, strawberry, 208.
Alternaria spp., castor bean, 332.
    Cornus asperifolia, 339.
    cotton, 325, 326.
    flax, 228.
    garden beet, 253.
    Hydrangea sp., 364.
    Jussiaea decurrens, 365.
    pepper, 260.
    summer squash, 269.
    tobacco, 330.
    tomato, 192, 275.
  blight, pea, 283.
  brassicae, Brassica oleracea var.
      broccoli, 254.
    cabbage, 256.
    cauliflower, 255.
    turnip, 259.
  carotae, carrot, 270.
  cucumerina, cantaloupe, 263.
    cucumber, 265.
    squash, 267.
    watermelon, 262.
  dianthi, Dianthus caryophyllus,
    358.
  herculea, cabbage, 256.
    cauliflower, 255.
    radish, 285.
  radicina, carrot, 270.
  solani, eggplant, 286.
    pepper, 260.
    potato, 191, 237.
    tomato, 194, 274.
  tenuis, Bryophyllum pinnatum, 353.
  tomato, tomato, 194, 274.
Anguina tritici, wheat, 230.
Angular yellow spot, peach, 299.
Aphanomyces cochlioides, sugar beet,
    333.
  euteiches, pea, 283.
Aphelenchoides fragariae,
    Chrysanthemum spp., 356.
  fragariae, strawberry, 208, 301.
Arachnopeziza aurelia, Quercus sp.,
    342.

Armillaria mellea, Acer spp., 336.
    black oak, 342.
    cherry, 313.
    Genistra sp., 361.
    mountain ash, 342.
    Norway maple, 342.
    Paeonia spp., 368.
    peach, 295.
    Rosa spp., 372.
    sugar maple, 342.
    Thuja spp., 349.
Ascochyta sp., Clematis spp., 356.
    Erica sp., 359.
    green peas, 198, 199.
    pea, 284.
    white sweet clover, 240.
  caulicola, sweet clover, 240.
  graminicola, barley, 226.
  imperfecta, alfalfa, 238.
  lethalis, sweet clover, 240.
  pinodella, pea, 284.
  pinodella, vetch, 242.
  pisi, pea, 284, see also Mycosphae-
    rella pinodes.
  rhei, rhubarb, 286.
Asia, eastern, host index of plant
    pathogens and virus diseases
    in, 93-123.
Aspergillus spp., cotton, 325.
  field corn, 234.
  sweetpotato, 271.
  niger, field corn, 234
    grape, 322.
    onion, 248.
  ochraceus, field corn, 234.
Asperisporium caricae, papaya, 300.
Aster yellows (virus), Calendula
    officinalis, 354.
    celery, 252.
    lettuce, 273.
Atropellis piniphila, Pinus ponderosa,
    348.

B

Bacillus sp., sugar beet, 333.
Bacteria, in Hawaii and their hosts,
    76-77.
Bacterial wilt, tobacco, 202.
Bacterium dissolvens, see Erwinia
    carotovora.

Bacterium mori, see Phytomonas mori.
Baldwin spot, apple, see bitter pit.
Basidiophora entospora, Callistephus
    chinensis, 354.
Big vein (virus), lettuce, 273.
Bitter pit (non-par.), apple, 310.
Black bundle, corn, 187.
Black-end (non-par.), pear, 318.
Black heart (non-par.), celery, 252.
Black leaf spot, Diospyros spp.,
    339.
Black ring (virus), Brassica oleracea
    var. broccoli, 255.
    Brassica oleracea var. italica,
    255.
    cauliflower, 256.
Black root and root rot (undet),
    strawberry, 208, 304.
Black spot (non-par.), garden beet,
    253.
Blakemore yellows, see leaf
    variegation.
Blast (non-par.), oats, 185, 226.
Blight, hops, 328.
Blight (bacterial), Ulmus parvi-
    folia, 345.
Blight (non-par.), garden beet,
    253.
Blight (undet.), Matthiola spp.,
    367.
Blight and dieback (undet.), Thuja
    spp., 349.
Blossom blight (non-par.), cherry,
    315.
Blossom-end rot (non-par.), pepper,
    261.
    tomato, 193, 195, 278.
Blotchy ripening (non-par.), tomato,
    278.
Blue-green algae, blue grass, 242.
    clover, 242.
Botryosphaeria ribis, red currant,
    319.
Botryosporium pulchrum, tomato, 275.
Botrytis sp., Antirrhinum majus, 351.
    Delphinium spp., 357.
    Dianthus caryophyllus, 358.
    grape, 322.
    Lilium spp., 366.
    onion, 248.

Botrytis sp., Paeonia spp., 368.
    allii, onion, 248.
    cinerea, Euphorbia spp., 360.
        Gladiolus spp., 362.
        lettuce, 272.
        Lilium spp., 366.
        strawberry, 302.
    elliptica, Lilium spp., 366.
    tulipae, Tulipa spp., 376.
Boydia insculpta, Ilex spp., 340.
Breaking of blossoms, Dianthus
    caryophyllus, 359.
Bremia lactucae, lettuce, 272.
    Sonchus oleraceus, 374.
Brown root rot (undet.), tobacco, 332.
Bubakia crotonis, Croton monanthogynus,
    357.
Bumpy peach (virus), peach, 298.
Bunchy top, eggplant, 286.
    tomato, 279.

               C

Calico (undet.), peach, 299.
Canker, Boysenberry, 320.
    hops, 328.
Canker-stain, London planetree, 340.
Capnodium sp., Citrus sinensis, 300.
    Pinus strobus, 348.
Cephalosporium sp., Diospyros spp.,
    339.
    acremonium, corn, 187.
    field corn, 234.
Ceratostomella sp., London planetree,
    341.
    Platanus occidentalis, 341.
    fimbriata, sweetpotato, 189, 271.
    ulmi, Ulmus spp., 344.
Cercospora sp., Ambrosia trifida, 350.
    Catalpa spp., 338.
    Hibiscus rosa-sinensis, 363.
    Hymenocallis occidentalis, 364.
    peanut, 325.
    strawberry, 302.
    Vernonia baldwinii, 376.
    Viburnum spp., 376.
    acalyphae, Acalypha ostryaefolia,
    350.
    althaeina, Althaea rosea, 350.
    cotton, 326.

Cercospora antipus, Lonicera sp., 366.
    apii, celery, 250.
    apii carotae, carrot, 270.
    apii-pastinacae, parsnip, 280.
    arborescentis, Hydrangea arbores-
        cens, 364.
    asparagi, asparagus, 252.
    beticola, Beta vulgaris macrorhiza,
        254.
        garden beet, 253.
        sugar beet, 200, 333.
    capsici, pepper, 260.
    catalpae, Catalpa spp., 338.
    chenopodii, Chenopodium hybridum,
        355.
    citrullina, watermelon, 262.
    cruenta, cowpea, 242.
    flagellaris, Phytolacca americana,
        370.
    fusca, pecan, 324.
    gaurae, Gaura biennis, 361.
    medicagini , alfalfa, 238.
    meliae, Melia azedarach, 367.
    minim , pear, 317.
    moricola, Morus alba, 311.
    nicotianae, tobacco, 330.
    oryzae. rice, 228.
    pachypus, Helianthus spp., 363.
    personata, peanut, 325.
    pittospori, Pittosporum spp., 371.
    rhododendri, Rhododendron
        catawbiense, 372.
    ricinella, castor bean, 332.
    rosicola, Rosa spp., 372.
    rosigena, Rosa spp., 372.
    smilacina, Smilax bona-nox, 374.
    sorghi, Sorghum halepense, 246.
    varia, Viburnum opulus, 376.
    variicolor, Paeonia spp., 369.
    vignae, cowpea, 242.
    violae, Viola spp., 377.
    zebrina, Trifolium hybridum, 241.
        Trifolium pratense, 241.
Cercosporella albo-maculans,
        Brassica chinensis, 254.
    petsai cabbage, 259.
    turnip, 259.
    herpotrichoides, wheat, 230, 231.
    pastinacae, parsnip, 280.
    rubi, blackberry, 319.

Cercosporella rubi, dewberry, 320.
Cerebella andropogonis, Axonopus
        compressus, 244.
    Tricholaena repens, 247.
Check list of fungi, bacteria, nematodes,
        and viruses occurring in
        Hawaii, 1-91.
Chlorosis, Buxus sempervirens , 354.
    Camellia japonica, 355.
    Catalpa spp., 338.
    cherry, 315.
    Choisya ternata, 356.
    Citrus grandis, 300.
    Citrus sinensis, 300.
    cowpea, 243.
    Gladiolus spp., 262.
    huckleberry, 304.
    Ilex spp., 340.
    Italian prune, 313.
    Ligustrum spp., 366.
    peach, 206.
    peanut, 325.
    Quercus palustris, 343.
    Rosa spp., 373.
    sour cherry, 315.
    Spiraea spp., 374.
    sweet cherry, 315.
    Thuja spp., 349.
Choanephora sp., Hibiscus spp., 363.
    conjuncta, cotton, 326.
    Ipomoea spp., 364.
    okra, 271.
    pea, 284.
    Petunia spp., 370.
    cucurbitarum, cowpea, 242.
    okra, 271.
Cintractia subinclusa, Carex rostrata,
        355.
Cladosporium, grape, 322.
    carpophilum, peach, 206, 295.
        plum, 316,
    cucumerinum. cantaloupe, 263.
        squash, 267.
        summer squash, 269.
    effusum, pecan, 324.
    fulvum, tomato, 275.
    herbarum, pepper, 260.
    paeoniae, Paeonia spp., 369.
    pisicola, pea, 284.
Claviceps sp., Agropyron smithii, 243.
    Agropyron trachycaulum, 243.

Claviceps sp., Elymus spp., 245.
purpurea, Agropyron repens, 243.
  Agropyron spicatum, 243.
  barley, 226.
  rye, 182, 229.
  wheat, 230.
Clitocybe tabescens, tung-oil tree, 325.
Coccomyces hiemalis, cherry, 207, 313.
  lutescens, chokecherry, 335.
  prunophorae, plum, 316.
Cold injury, tobacco, 332.
Coleosporium solidaginis, Callistephus chinensis, 354.
  Pinus resinosa, 348.
Colletotrichum sp., African succulent Euphorbias, 360.
  Euphorbia fimbriata, 360.
  pepper, 260.
  antirrhini, Antirrhinum majus, 351.
  circinans, onion, 248.
  destructivum, alfalfa, 238.
    Melilotus alba, 240.
  falcatum, sugar cane, 334.
  fruit rot, tomato, 276.
  graminicolum, Agrostis alba, 243.
    alfalfa, 238.
    red and white clovers, 241.
    rye, 183, 229.
    Sorghum vulgare sudanense, 246.
    wheat, 231.
  hibisci, Hibiscus spp., 363.
  lagenarium, cantaloupe, 263.
    cucumber, 266.
    squash, 267.
    watermelon, 262.
  lindemuthianum, bean, 196, 281.
    cowpea, 242.
    green beans, 196.
  lini, flax, 228.
  nigrum, pepper, 260.
  phomoides, tomato, 275.
  spinaciae, spinach, 293.
  trifolii, alfalfa, 238.
  violae-tricoloris, Viola papilionacea, 377.
Coniothyrium sp., Ulmus spp., 344.
  concentricum, Yucca filamentosa, 377.
Coniothyrium wernsdorffiae, Rosa spp., 372.
Copper injury, cherry, 315.
Copper russetting, apple, 311.
Cork (non-par.), apple, 310.
  cherry, 315.
Corticium microsclerotia, fig, 301.
  sasakii, Cynodon dactylon, 244.
  solani, bean, 281.
    cabbage, 256.
    cauliflower, 255.
    Cichorium endivia, 261.
    cotton, 326.
    lettuce, 272.
    potato, 287.
    sweetpotato, 271.
    tomato, 275.
  stevensii, fig, 301.
    Pittosporum spp., 371.
Coryneum beijerinckii, almond, 324.
  apricot, 312.
  peach, 295.
  prune, 312.
  Prunus emarginata, 314.
  sweet cherry, 314.
  cardinale, Monterey cypress, 346.
Cracked stem (non-par.), celery, 252.
Cracking (non-par.), cherry, 315.
Crazy top, almond, 324.
  cotton, 327.
Crinkle (virus), Pelargonium snp., 369.
  strawberry, 208, 304.
Crinkle leaf, cotton, 327.
Cronartium sp., Quercus alba, 336.
  Quercus macrocarpa, 336.
  Quercus rubra, 336.
  cerebrum, Pinus banksiana, 348.
  comptoniae, Pinus spp., 348.
  harknessii, Pinus ponderosa, 348.
  quercuum, Pinus spp., 348.
  ribicola, black currant, 319.
    currant, 319.
    gooseberry, 318.
    Ribes, 348, 372.
    white pine, 348, 372.
Crown and shoot rot, milo, see milo disease.
Crown girdle (undet.), pear, 318.
  tung-oil tree, 325.
Crown rot (undet.), garden beet, 254.

384

Cryptosporella viticola, grape, 323.
Cucumber mosaic (virus), celery, 252.
    sweet pepper, 261.
Cumminsiella sanguinea, Berberis
      aquifolium, 353.
Curly top (virus), bean, 283.
    Beta vulgaris macrorhiza, 254.
    cantaloupe, 265.
    cucumber, 267.
    dry beans, 197.
    garden beet, 253.
    pepper, 261.
    potato, 291.
    squash, 268.
    sugar beet, 200, 334.
    swiss chard, 254.
    tomato, 193, 195, 278.
Curvularia lunata, rice, 228.
Cuscuta sp., Ambrosia trifida, 350.
    Antirrhinum majus, 351.
    eggplant, 286.
    Helianthus spp., 363.
    tomato, 275.
    arvensis, alfalfa, 238.
Cutting rot, Azalea spp., 353.
Cyanospora albicedrae, Juniperus
      mexicana, 347.
Cycloconium oleaginum, olive, 312.
Cylindrosporium sp., Amorpha fruti-
      cosa, 351.
    Fraxinus spp., 340.
    Fraxinus toumeyi, 340.
    consociatum, Acer glabrum, 336.
    filipendulae, Spiraea spp., 374.
    griseum, Sapindus drummondii, 373.
    montenegrinum, Trollius albiflorus,
      376.
    oculatum, Populus deltoides, 341.
    spiraeicola, Spiraea lucida, 374.
Cytospora sp., Acer spp., 336.
    Picea spp., 347.
    Picea pungens, 347.
    Populus spp., 341.
    Ulmus spp., 344.
    chrysosperma, Populus spp., 341.
    Salix spp., 343.
    sacchari, sugar cane, 334.

D

Damping-off, broadleaves, 335.
    conifers, 335.

Damping-off, Pinus ponderosa, 335, 346.
    Pinus resinosa, 346.
    sugar beet, 200.
Dark center (non-par.), turnip, 259.
Dasyscypha sp., Pseudotsuga taxifolia,
    348.
Dead hills, hops, 328.
Deficiency diseases, cotton, 201, 327.
    tobacco, 202.
Dendrophoma obscurans, strawberry, 302.
Diachea leucopoda, strawberry, 302.
Diamond canker (undet.), prune, 313.
Diaporthe batatatis, sweetpotato, 271.
    phaseolorum, lima bean, 280.
    sojae, soybean, 240.
Dibotryon morbosum, cherry, 314.
    prune, 313.
    Prunus maritima, 316.
Didymella applanata, raspberry, 320.
Didymellina macrospora, Iris sp., 364.
Dieback, Azalea spp., 353.
    Boysenberry, 320.
    Calluna vulgaris, 355.
    cherry, 315.
    filbert, 324.
    prune, 313.
    Robinia pseudoacacia, 343.
    Rosa spp., 373.
    Taxus cuspidata, 349.
Diplocarpon earliana, strawberry, 208,
    302.
    rosae, Rosa spp., 373.
Diplodia sp., Allium sativum, 250.
    corn, 186, 187, 233.
    Rosa spp., 373.
    sweet corn, 188, 237.
    caryogena, Carya cordiformis, 338.
    gossypina, cotton, 325, 326.
    longispora, Quercus prinus, 342.
    natalensis, Citrus limonia, 300.
    tubericola, sweetpotato, 272.
    zeae, corn, 186, 187.
Discosia artocreas, Cercis canadensis,
    339.
Ditylenchus dipsaci, alfalfa, 238.
    Allium sativum, 250.
    narcissus, 140.
    onion, 248.
    strawberry, 302.
Dormant hills, hops, 328.
Dothichiza populea, Populus spp., 341.

Dothiorella sp., tung-oil tree, 325.
  ulmi, Ulmus spp., 344.
Drought injury, birch, 338.
  cabbage, 256.
  cherry, 315.
  field corn, 237.
  horsechestnut, 337.
  ornamental trees and shrubs,
    336.
  pea, 285.
  peach, 300.
  pear, 318.
  Picea spp., 348.
  Pinus sylvestris, 348.
  wheat, 233.
Drought and heat injury, oats, 226.
  potato, 293.
  strawberry, 304.
Drought spot (non-par.), prune, 313.
Dwarf, strawberry, 208.

E

Ear rots, corn, 186, 187, 234.
Elsinoe ampelina, grape, 323.
  veneta, blackberry, 319.
    Boysenberry, 320.
    dewberry, 320.
    raspberry, 320.
    youngberry, 322.
Elytroderma deformans, Pinus
    ponderosa, 348.
Endothia parasitica, chestnut, 338.
Entomosporium sp., crabapple, 336.
    hawthorn, 336.
    thuemenii, Crataegus spp., 339.
Entyloma sp., Physalis sp., 370.
  dahliae, Dahlia snp., 357.
  nymphaea, Nymphaea odorata, 368.
  oryzae, rice, 228.
Erwinia amylovora, apple, 204, 205,
    304.
    Crataegus spp., 339.
    pear, 203, 317.
    Pyracantha sp., 371.
    quince, 301.
  aroideae, Delphinium spp., 358.
    Zantedeschia sp., 377.
  carotovora, Brussels sprouts, 259.
    cabbage, 257.
    carrot, 270.

Erwinia carotovora, cauliflower, 255.
    celery, 251.
    field corn, 235.
    Iris sp., 364.
    onion, 248.
    potato, 287.
    squash, 268.
    tobacco, 330.
    tomato, 275.
  lapsa, field corn, 235.
    sorghum, 230.
  phytophthora, potato, 190, 288.
  tracheiphila, cantaloupe, 264.
    cucumber, 266.
    watermelon, 262.
    winter squash, 268.
Erysiphe sp., Euphorbia sp., 360.
  cichoracearum, cantaloupe, 264.
    cucumber, 266.
    Helianthus spp., 363.
    Phlox spp., 370.
    salsify, 294.
    squash, 268.
    sunflower, 238.
    Taraxacum spp., 375.
    winter squash, 268.
    Zinnia elegans, 377.
  graminis, barley, 181, 226.
    Dactylis glomerata, 245.
    oats, 225.
    rye, 229.
    turnip, 259.
    wheat, 231.
  polygoni, bean, 281.
    Brassica oleracea var. napo-
      brassica, 254.
    cabbage, 257.
    cowpea, 242.
    Delphinium spp., 358.
    green beans, 196.
    pea, 284.
    Phaseolus aureus, 280.
    Polygonum buxiforme, 371.
    red clover, 241.
Exobasidium burtii, Azalea spp., 352.
  vaccinii, Azalea spp., 352.
Exosporium concentricum, Euonymus
    japonica, 360.
F
Fabraea sp., crabapple, 336.

Fabraea sp., hawthorn, 336.
  maculata, Crataegus spp., 339.
    pear, 203, 317.
    quince, 301.
False blossom (virus), cranberry,
    322.
Fasciation, yew, see witches'
    broom.
Filiform mosaic (cucurbit virus),
    tomato, 279.
Fomes sp., horsechestnut, 337.
  annosus, Kalmia latifolia, 365.
    Picea spp., 347.
  applanatus, Robinia pseudoacacia,
    343.
  fraxinophilus, Fraxinus lanceolata,
    340.
  igniarius, Salix spp., 343.
Foot rots, corn, 186, 187, 236.
  rye, 183.
  wheat, 178, 179.
Frenching (non-par.), tobacco, 332.
Frost injury, apple, 311.
  cherry, 315.
  peach, 300.
  pear, 318.
  plum, 317.
  prune, 313.
  Syringa vulgaris, 375.
Frost killing, Abies concolor, 335.
  broadleaves, 335.
  conifers, 335.
  Pseudotsuga taxifolia, 335.
Fruit gumming (non-par.), peach, 299.
Fruit pox, tomato, 278.
Fruit rots, strawberry, 208.
  tomato, 192, 194.
Fumago spp., Ilex spp., 340.
  Quercus spp., 342.
  vagans, Fagus spp., 339.
Fungi, of Mount Shasta, California,
    host index to, 125-133.
  in Hawaii and their hosts, 37-
    76.
Fusarium sp., Agrostis spp., 243.
  asparagus, 252.
  barley, 180.
  bean, 281.
  cantaloupe, 264.
  celery, 251.

Fusarium spp., cotton, 325, 326.
  Dahlia spp., 357.
  Dianthus caryophyllus, 358.
  field corn, 235, 236.
  Freesia sp., 361.
  Gladiolus spp., 362.
  green peas, 198, 199.
  Iris kaempferi, 364.
  Narcissus sp., 367.
  oats, 225.
  onion, 248.
  pea, 283, 284.
  Pelargonium spp., 369.
  pepper, 260.
  potato, 190, 288.
  Primula sp., 371.
  sorghum, 230.
  spinach, 293.
  summer squash, 269.
  sweet corn, 188, 237.
  sweetpotato, 272.
  Taxus cuspidata, 349.
  tobacco, 330.
  wheat, 231.
  white sweet clover, 240.
  winter squash, 269.
  Zucchini squash, 269.
  apii, celery, 251.
  apii pallidum, celery, 251.
  avenaceum, peach, 295.
    potato, 288.
  bulbigenum batatas, sweetpotato,
    139, 272.
  bulbigenum lycopersici, tomato, 192
    194, 275.
  bulbigenum niveum, watermelon, 262.
  bulbigenum niveum f.2, cantaloupe,
    264.
  bulbigenum tracheiphilum, cowpea, 2
  conglutinans, cabbage, 257.
    cauliflower, 255.
    callistephi, Callistephus
    chinensis, 354.
  heterosporium, Axonopus compressus,
    244.
  javanicum, summer squash, 269.
  lini, flax, 228.
  moniliforme, cotton, 325, 326.
    field corn, 235.
    sugar cane, 334.

Fusarium nivale, Agrostis spp., 243.
  orthoceras longius, strawberry,
    302.
  orthoceras pisi, pea, 284.
  oxysporum, sweetpotato, 189, 272.
  oxysporum f.1, potato, 288.
  oxysporum f.2., sweetpotato, 189,
    272.
  oxysporum f.8, pea, 284.
  oxysporum gladioli, Gladiolus
    spp., 362.
  oxysporum medicaginis, alfalfa,
    238.
  oxysporum nicotianae, tobacco,
    330.
  perniciosum, mimosa, 337.
  radicicola, potato, 288.
  root rot, carrot, 270.
  solani eumartii, potato, 288.
  solani var. martii f.2, pea, 283.
  solani var. martii f.3, bean, 281.
  spinaciae, spinach, 293.
  vasinfectum, cotton, 201, 325,
    326.
  vasinfectum zonatum f.1, onion,
    248.
  wilt, casaba melon, 265.
    cotton, 146, 147.
    honeydew melon, 265.
Fusicladium eriobotryae, loquat,
    301.
  saliciperdum, Salix spp., 343.
  tremulae, Populus spp., 341.
Fusicoccum sp., Pyracantha sp., 371.
Fusisporium rubi, dewberry, 321.
  raspberry, 321.

G

Ganoderma sp., Colutea arborescens,
    356.
Gibberella spp., field corn, 236.
  sweet corn, 237.
  saubinetii, see G. zeae.
  zeae, barley, 181, 226.
    field corn, 235.
    oats, 225.
    rye, 229.
    wheat, 178, 179, 231.
Girdle (non-par.), garden beet, 253.

Gloeodes pomigena, apple, 305.
  pear, 317.
Gloeosporium spp., Acer spp., 336.
  Nephthytis sp., 368.
  Rosa spp., 373.
  apocryptum, Acer spp., 336.
  catalpae, Catalpa spp., 338.
  fagi, Fagus spp., 339.
  perennans, apple, see Neofabraea
    perennans.
  ulmi, Ulmus americana, 344.
  Ulmus pumila, 344.
Glomerella cingulata, apple, 204, 205,
    305.
  Ligustrum spp., 366.
  pepper, 260.
  Symphoricarpos spp., 374.
  gossypii, cotton, 201, 325, 326.
  piperata, pepper, 260.
Gnomonia leptostyla, black walnut, 340.
  ulmea, Ulmus spp., 344.
  veneta, Platanus spp., 341.
  Quercus spp., 342.
  sycamore, 342.
Graphiola phoenicis, Phoenix sp., 370.
  Phoenix canariensis, 370.
Green mosaic (virus), sugar cane, 334.
Greene mottle, apple, 310.
Guignardia aesouli, horsechestnut, 337.
  bidwellii, grape, 209, 323.
    Parthenocissus quinquefolia, 369.
    Parthenocissus tricuspidata, 369.
  vaccinii, cranberry, 322.
Gymnoconia peckiana, black raspberry,
    320.
  blackberry, 319.
  wild blackberry, 319.
Gymnosporangium sp., Amelanchier sp.,
    350.
  apple, 204, 205, 306.
  Crataegus spp., 336, 339.
  Juniperus monosperma, 347.
  Malus spp., 336.
  betheli, Juniperus scopulorum, 347.
  clavariaeforme, Juniperus communis
    depressa, 347.
  clavipes, apple, 305.
    Crataegus spp., 339.
    flowering crab, 340.
    Juniperus spp., 347.

Gymnosporangium clavipes, quince,
    301.
    exiguum, Juniperus mexicana, 347.
    floriforme, Juniperus spp., 347.
    globosum, apple, 306.
        Crataegus spp., 339.
        Juniperus spp., 346, 347.
    juniperi-virginianae, apple, 306.
    juniperi-virginianae, flowering
        crab, 340.
        Juniperus spp., 346, 347.
        Juniperus chinensis, 347.
    juniperinum, Juniperus communis
        depressa, 347.
    nelsoni, Juniperus spp., 347.

                    H

Hail injury, pear, 318.
    prune, 313.
Hair sprout, potato, 291.
Hawaii, check list of fungi, bacteria,
            nematodes, and viruses in,
            1-91.
Heart rot, sugar beet, 334.
Heart canker, flax, 228.
Heat injury, cabbage, 256.
    field corn, 237.
    pea, 285.
    Tsuga spp., 349.
    wheat, 233.
Helminthosporium spp., Agrostis spp.,
            243.
    Allium sativum, 250.
    barley, 180.
    field corn, 236.
    Poa spp., 246.
    Stenotaphrum secundatum, 246.
    undetermined Gramineae, 247.
    wheat, 231.
    avenae, oats, 225.
    bromi, Bromus spp., 244.
    foot rot, barley 180.
    gramineum, barley, 180, 227.
    oryzae, see Ophiobolus miyabeanus.
    papulosum, apple, 306.
    sativum, barley, 227.
        wheat, 231.
    turcicum, corn, 187.
        field corn, 236.

Helminthosporium turcicum, sorghum,
    230.
    Sorghum vulgare sudanense, 246.
    sweet corn, 237.
Heterodera marioni, Althaea rosea, 350.
    American-Egyptian cotton, 143.
    Antirrhinum majus, 351.
    bean, 138, 147, 281.
    Brabham peas, 139.
    cantaloupe, 264.
    carrot, 270.
    celery, 251.
    chemical treatment of soil, 150.
    Chinese lily, 141.
    cigar-wrapper tobacco, 143.
    clover, 241.
    corn, 139.
    cotton, 139, 146, 201, 326.
    cowpea, 138, 139, 242.
    crop plants, 142.
    cucumber, 266.
    effect of crop rotation, 145.
    eggplant, 286.
    Euonymus spp., 360.
    Gardenia jasminoides, 361.
    Gelsemium sempervirens, 361.
    Gladiolus spp., 362.
    globe artichoke, 269.
    grasses, 143.
    hops, 329.
    huckleberry, 304.
    Ipomoea purpurea, 364.
    Lespedeza stipulacea, 139.
    lettuce, 273.
    Ligustrum spp., 366.
    Ligustrum lucidum compactum, 366.
    lima bean, 139.
    Nancy Hall sweet potato, 141.
    Nicotiana spp., 140.
    okra, 271.
    Paeonia spp., 369.
    Paper White narcissus, 141.
    pea, 284.
    peach, 296.
    peanut, 139.
    Petunia spp., 370.
    Pinus lambertiana, 139.
    potato, 142, 145, 288.
    resistance in Nicotiana, 139.
    Rosa spp., 373.

Heterodera marioni, snap bean, 139.
   soybean, 139.
   strawberry, 302.
   sweetpotato, 272.
   tobacco, 145, 330.
   tomato, 139, 141, 146, 149, 192, 276.
   turnip, 259.
   Ulmus spp., 345.
   Viburnum spp., 376.
   Viola spp., 377.
   watermelon, 150, 262.
   weeds, 142.
  marioni infestation, 148.
Heterosporium echinulatum, Dianthus caryophyllus, 358.
  gracile, Belamcanda chinensis, 353.
   Iris sp., see Didymellina macrospora.
  phlei, Phleum pratense, 246.
  variabile, spinach, 293.
Hopperburn (leafhopper), potato, 191, 292.
Host index; fungi of Mount Shasta, California, 125-133.
  plant pathogens and virus diseases, eastern Asia, 92-123.
Hyalopsora polypodii, Cystopteris sp., 357.
Hypodermella nervisequia, Pseudotsuga taxifolia, 348.
Hypoxylon sp., Platanus occidentalis, 341.
  atropunctata, Quercus spp., 342.

I

Index, host, fungi of Mount Shasta, California, 125-133.
  plant pathogens and virus diseases, eastern Asia, 93-123.
Internal breakdown, apple, 310.
Internal cork (non-par.), apple, 310.
Interveinal chlorosis (non-par.), chestnut, 338.

K

Kabatiella caulivora, clover, 241.
Kuehneola uredinis, blackberry, 319.

L

Leaf blight (non-par.), Arbutus menziesii, 337.
Leaf blotch (sterile fungus), rice, 229.
Leaf cast, Abies spp., 346.
Leaf-casting yellows (virus), peach, 298.
Leaf curl (undet.), prune, 313.
Leaf curl (virus), raspberry, 322.
Leaf drop, prune, 313.
  Robinia pseudoacacia, 343.
Leaf mottle, Fagus spp., 339.
Leaf necrosis (undet.), turnip, 259.
Leafroll (virus), potato, 190, 291.
Leaf scorch, Acer spp., 337.
  Fagus spp., 340.
  prune, 313.
Leaf scorch and blight (non-par.), Pseudotsuga taxifolia, 349.
Leaf spot (non-par.), Camellia japonica, 355.
  Phleum pratense, 246.
Leaf spotting (undet.), prune, 313.
Leaf spotting and defoliation (undet.), peach, 299.
Leaf variegation, strawberry, 208, 303.
Leptosphaeria coniothyrium, blackberry, 319.
  Boysenberry, 320.
  dewberry, 320.
  gooseberry, 318.
  raspberry, 321.
  Rosa spp., 373.
  youngberry, 322.
Leptosphaeria salvinii, rice, 228.
Leptothyrium acerinum, Acer saccharum, 336.
  periclymeni, Lonicera sp., 366.
  pomi, apple, 306.
  pear, 317.
Lime sulfur injury, cherry, 315.
Little peach (virus), peach, 298.
Lophodermium sp., Rhododendron spp., 372.

Lophodermium pinastri, Pinus spp.,
    348.
    rhododendri, Rhododendron
        catawoiense, 372.
Lycogala epidendrum, Pinus spp.,
    348.

M

Macrophoma candollei, Buxus semper-
        virens, 354.
    negundinis, Acer negundo, 337.
    nervicola, Quercus spp., 342.
    phlei, Phleum pratense, 246.
Macrophomina phaseoli, bean, 281.
    cowpea, 242.
    honevdew melon, 265.
    Persian melon, 265.
    Strophostyles helvola, 241.
Macrosporium sp., Dahlia sp., 357.
    onion, 248.
    catalpae, Catalpa spp., 338.
    porri, onion, 248.
    sarcinula parasiticum, onion, 249.
Malformation, Italian prune, 313.
Malnutrition (non-par.), cauliflower,
        256.
Marasmius tritici, Agrostis alba, 244.
    wheat, 231.
Marginal chlorosis (non-par.), chest-
        nut, 338.
Marssonia sp., crabapple, 336.
    green ash, 335.
    hawthorn, 336.
    fraxini, see Piggotia fraxini.
    juglandis, Juglans spp., 340.
Marssonina sp., Salix spp., 343.
    kriegeriana, Salix exigua, 343.
    panattoniana, lettuce, 273.
    populi, Populus alba, 341.
    Populus tremuloides, 335, 336.
Measles (non-par.), apple, 310.
Melampsora spp., cottonwood, 335.
    Populus spp., 336, 341.
    Populus balsamifera, 336.
    Populus candicans, 336.
    Populus carreiriana, 336.
Melampsora abietis-canadensis,
        Populus spp., 341.
Melampsora aecidioides, Populus
    alba, 341.

Melampsora bigelowii, Salix spp., 343.
    cassandrae, Picea spp., 348.
    lini, flax, 228.
    Linum lewisi, 228, 366.
    ribesii-purpureae, Salix sp., 343.
    Salix bebbiana, 343.
    Salix scouleriana, 343.
Melampsorella cerastii, Abies lasiocarpa
        346.
    Cerastium arvense, 355.
Melanopsichium austro-americanum,
    Polygonum lapathifolium, 371.
Micrococcus sp., undetermined Gramineae
    247.
Microorganisms and viruses, in Hawaii
        and their hosts, 38-82.
Microsphaera sp., Euonymus spp., 360.
    Symphoricarpos spp., 374.
Microsphaera alni, pecan, 324.
    Syringa vulgaris, 375.
    alni vaccinii, Catalpa spp., 338.
    diffusa, Symphoricarpos spp., 374.
    polonica, Hydrangea sp., 364.
Mild mosaic (virus), potato, 292.
Milo disease, reaction of sorghum
        varieties and hybrids to,
        165-175.
Missing hills, hops, 328.
Monilochaetes infuscans, sweetpotato,
        189, 272.
Mosaic (virus), alfalfa, 240.
    bean, 283.
    black raspberry, 322.
    Boysenberry, 320.
    cabbage, 259.
    Callicarpa americana, 354.
    cantaloupe, 265.
    cauliflower, 256.
    clover, 242.
    cowpea, 243.
    cucumber, 267.
    currant, 319.
    Dahlia spp., 357.
    dry beans, 197.
    eggplant, 287.
    garden beet, 253.
    Gladiolus spp., 262.
    green beans, 196.
    green peas, 198.
    Iris sp., 364.
    Lathyrus odoratus, 366.

Mosaic (virus), lettuce, 274.
  Lilium spp., 366.
  lima bean, 280.
  Melilotus alba, 240.
  Narcissus sp., 367.
  Ornithogalum aureum, 368.
  Paeonia spp., 369.
  pea, 285.
  peach, 298.
  Pelargonium spp., 370.
  pepper, 261.
  Petunia spp., 370.
  Phytolacca americana, 370.
  potato, 190.
  prune, 313.
  purple raspberry, 322.
  red raspberry, 322.
  Rosa spp., 373.
  Senecio cruentus, 374.
  soybean, 240.
  spinach, 294.
  squash, 268.
  strawberry, 304.
  sugar cane, 334.
  summer squash, 269.
  sweetpotato, 272.
  Tigridia sp., 375.
  tobacco, 202, 332.
  tomato, 193, 195, 279.
  turnip, 260.
  watermelon, 263.
  wheat, 233.
  winter squash, 269.
  Zinnia elegans, 377.
Mottle leaf (virus), cherry, 315.
Mount Shasta, California, host
        index to fungi of, 125-133.
Mucor spp., field corn, 236.
Multiple bud (undet.), sugar cane,
        334.
Mycosphaerella sp., tomato, 276.
  brassicicola, Brassica oleracea
        var. broccoli, 254.
    Brussels sprouts, 259.
    cabbage, 257.
    cauliflower, 255.
  cercidicola, Cercis canadensis,
        339.
  citrullina, watermelon, 262.
    winter squash, 269.
  fragariae, strawberry, 208, 302.

Mycosphaerella pinodes, green peas,
        198, 199.
    pea, 284.
  pomi, apple, 307.
  rosicola, Rosa spp., 373.
  rubi, blackberry, 319.
    Boysenberry, 320.
    raspberry, 321.
    youngberry, 322.
  rubina, raspberry, 320, 321.
    red raspberry, 321.
  sentina, pear, 317.

N

Naucoria cerealis, wheat, 231.
Necrosis, tomato, 279.
Nectria sp., Abies balsamea, 346.
    Abies concolor, 346.
    horsechestnut, 337.
    ornamentals, 349.
    Ulmus spp., 345.
  cinnabarina, currant, 319.
    Fagus spp., 339.
    Ligustrum amurense, 366.
    Ulmus spp., 345.
  ditissima, Acer spp., 337.
  rousselliana, Buxus sempervirens, 354.
Nematode conference, proceedings third
        national plant, 135-150.
Nematodes, Citrus sinensis, 300.
    in Hawaii and their hosts, 76-82.
Neofabraea malicorticis, apple, 307.
  perennans, apple, 307.
Net necrosis (virus), potato, 291.
Nigrospora sphaerica, field corn, 235.
Nummularia discreta, apple, 307.

O

Oidium sp., Hydrangea sp., 364.
  caricae, papaya, 300.
Oil injury, apple, 311.
Ophiobolus graminis, barley, 180.
    wheat, 231.
  miyabeanus, rice, 229.
Ovularia asteris, Aster engelmanni,
        352.
  obliqua, Rumex sp., 373.
Ovulinia azaleae, Azalea spp., 352.

P

Penicillium sp., Citrus spp., 300.
  cotton, 325, 326.
  cranberry, 322.
  field corn, 235, 236.
  prune, 313.
  Tulipa spp., 376.
  expansum, apple, 307.
  pear, 318.
  gladioli, Gladiolus spp., 362.
Peronospora sp., Eriogonum blissianum, 360.
  Teucrium canadense, 375.
  antirrhini, Antirrhinum majus,351.
  destructor, onion, 249.
  effusa, Chenopodium album, 355.
  spinach, 294.
  lamii, Lamium amplexicaule, 365.
  manshurica, soybean, 240.
  parasitica, cabbage, 257.
    Capsella bursa-pastoris, 355.
  cauliflower, 255.
  radish, 285.
  pisi, pea, 284.
  potentillae, Geum sp., 361.
  potentillae, Potentilla gracilis ssp. nuttallii, 371.
  schachtii, garden beet, 253.
    sugar beet, 333.
  tabacina, tobacco, 202, 330.
  trifoliorum, alfalfa, 238.
Pestalotia sp., Rhododendron spp.,372.
  guepini, Rhododendron spp.,372.
Pestalozzia funerea, Thuja spp., 349.
Pezicula carpinea, Carpinus caroliniana, 338.
Pezizella lythri, strawberry, 303.
Phaeocryptopus gäumanni, Pseudotsuga taxifolia, 348.
Phleospora aceris, Acer spp., 337.
  Acer saccharinum, 337.
  osmorrhizae, Osmorhiza divaricata, 368.
  Osmorhiza occidentalis, 368.
Phloem necrosis (virus), Ulmus spp., 345.
Phoma sp., peanut, 325.
  sugar beet, 333.
  betae, sugar beet, 333.

Phoma destructiva, tomato, 276.
  fruit rot, tomato, 276.
  lathyrina, cowpea, 242.
  lingam, cabbage, 257.
  turnip, 259.
Phoma persicae, peach, 296.
  terrestris, onion, 249.
Phomopsis sp., Ilex spp., 340.
  callistephi, Callistephus chinensis, 354.
  gardeniae, Gardenia jasminoides, 361.
  juniperovora, cedar, 346.
  eastern red cedar, 335.
  Juniperus spp., 347.
  sojae, see Diaporthe sojae.
  stewartii, Cosmos spp., 357.
  vexans, eggplant, 286.
Phony peach (virus), peach, 298.
Phoradendron flavescens, Ulmus spp.,345.
Phragmidium sp., Rosa spp., 373.
  americanum, Rosa setigera, 373.
  andersoni, Potentilla fruticosa, 371.
  ivesiae, Potentilla gracilis, 371.
    Potentilla gracilis ssp. nuttallii, 371.
    Potentilla nuttallii, 371.
  montivagum, Rosa sp., 373.
    Rosa nutkana, 373.
  potentillae, Potentilla flabelliformis, 371.
    Potentilla pensylvanica, 371.
  rosae-setigerae, Rosa spp., 373.
Phragmidium rubi-idaei, blackberry, 321.
  Rubus strigosus, 321.
  speciosum, Rosa spp., 373.
Phyllachora trifolii, Trifolium hybridum, 241.
  Trifolium pratense, 241.
  Trifolium repens, 241.
Phyllosticta spp., Acer spp., 337.
  Amaranthus retroflexus, 350.
  Buxus sempervirens, 354.
  Carpinus caroliniana, 338.
  Catalpa sp., 338.
  crabapple, 336.
  Fraxinus spp., 340.
  Fraxinus velutina, 340.
  hawthorn, 336.

Phyllosticta sp., Hedera spp., 363;
    Phlox spp., 370.
     Sassafras albidum, 344.
     Ulmus spp., 345.
   antirrhini, Antirrhinum majus, 351.
   bumeliae, Bumelia lanuginosa, 338, 353.
   catalpae, Catalpa spp., 338.
   celtidis, Celtis occidentalis, 338·
   gossypina, cotton, 326.
   hederaecola, Hedera helix, 363.
   ilicicola, Ilex spp., 340.
   kalmicola, Kalmia latifolia, 365.
   smilacis, Smilax glauca, 374.
   solitaria, apple, 204, 205, 307.
   straminella, rhubarb, 286.
   trollii, Trollius albiflorus, 376.
   viridis, Fraxinus americana, 340.
Phymatotrichum omnivorum, alfalfa, 239.
   apricot, 312.
   Aster spp., 352.
   Baccharis neglecta, 353;.
   Buxus sempervirens, 354.
   Cercis canadensis, 339.
   Chrysanthemum spp., 356.
   Cornus spp., 339.
   cotton, 201, 327.
   cowpea, 242.
   Elaeagnus argentea, 359.
   Euonymus spp., 360.
   fig, 301.
   Gelsemium sempervirens, 361.
   Hibiscus syriacus, 363.
   Juglans rupestris, 340.
   Lantana camara, 365.
   Lantana sellowiana, 365.
   Ligustrum sp., 366.
   Ligustrum amurense, 366.
   Ligustrum lucidum compactum, 366.
   Melia azedarach, 367.
   mulberry, 311.
   okra, 271.
   pear, 318.
   pecan, 324.
   peach 206, 296.
   Philadelphus grandiflorus, 370.

Phymatotrichum omnivorum, Populus spp., 341.
   Pyracantha sp., 372.
   Rhus spp., 343.
   Rosa spp., 373.
   Salix spp., 343.
   Spiraea spp., 374.
   sweet clover, 240.
   sweetpotato, 272.
   swiss chard, 254.
   Thuja orientalis, 349.
   tobacco, 331.
   tomato, 276.
   Ulmus americana, 345.
   Zinnia elegans, 377.
Physalospora astragali, Astragalus bisulcatus, 352.
   Astragalus goniatus, 352.
   obtusa, apple, 204, 205, 308.
Physarum spp., undetermined Gramineae, 247.
   cinereum, Cynodon dactylon, 244.
   Stenotaphrum secundatum, 246.
Physiological yellow leaf, cherry, 315.
Physoderma menyanthis, Menyanthes trifoliata, 367.
   zeae-maydis, field corn, 236.
Physopella fici, fig, 301.
Phytomonas spp., Dianthus caryophyllus, 358.
   dry beans, 197.
   green beans, 196.
   Syringa vulgaris, 375.
   tobacco, 202.
   aceris, Acer spp., 337.
   aleuritidis, tung-oil tree, 325.
   andropogoni, sorghum, 230.
   Sorghum vulgare sudanense, 246.
   angulata, tobacco, 331.
   atrofaciens, wheat, 231.
   begoniae, Begonia spp., 353.
   berberidis, Berberis spp., 353.
   campestris, Brassica oleracea var. broccoli, 254.
   Brassica oleracea var. napo-brassica, 254.
   cabbage, 258.
   cauliflower, 255.
   radish, 286.
   turnip, 259.

Phytomonas cerasi, Trifolium
    hybridum, 241.
    Trifolium pratense, 241.
    Trifolium repens, 241.
  coronafaciens, oats, 225.
  cucurbitae, squash, 268.
    winter squash, 269.
  delphinii, Delphinium spp., 358.
  fascians, Lathyrus odoratus,365.
  flaccumfaciens, bean, 281; 282.
  glycinea, soybean, 240.
  gummisudans, Gladiolus spp.,362.
  hederae, Hedera spp., 363.
  insidiosa, alfalfa, 239.
  jaggeri, celery, 251.
  lachrymans, cucumber, 266.
  maculicola, cabbage, 258.
    cauliflower, 255.
  malvacearum, cotton, 201, 327.
  marginata, Gladiolus spp., 362.
  medicaginis phaseolicola, bean,
    282.
    lima bean, 280.
  michiganensis, tomato, 193, 195,
    276.
  mori, Morus alba tatarica, 311.
    mulberry, 335.
  papavericola, Papaver spp., 369.
  papulans, apple, 308.
  pelargonii, Pelargonium spp., 369.
  phaseoli, bean, 282.
    lima bean, 280.
  pisi, green peas, 198.
    pea, 284.
  pruni, apricot, 312.
    cherry, 314.
    peach, 206, 296.
    plum, 316.
  rhizogenes, apple, 308.
    Rosa spp., 373.
  rubrilineans, sugar cane, 334.
  rubrisubalbricans, sugar cane,334.
  savastanoi, Nerium oleander, 368.
  sepedonica, potato, 191, 288.
  solanacearum, Dahlia spp., 357.
    potato, 191, 289.
    tobacco, 331.
    tomato, 276.
  stewartii, corn, 186, 187.
    field corn, 236.

Phytomonas stewartii, popcorn, 237.
    sweet corn, 188, 237.
  syringae, lima bean, 280.
    plum, 316.
    sweet cherry, 314.
    Syringa vulgaris, 375.
  tabaci, tobacco; 331.
  tardicrescens, Iris sp., 364.
  translucens, barley, 227.
  translucens undulosa, wheat, 231.
  tumefaciens, Althaea rosea, 350.
    apple, 308.
    black raspberry, 321.
    blackberry, 320.
    Boysenberry, 320.
    cotton, 327.
    Euonymus fortunei var. radicans,
      360.
    grape, 323.
    hops, 328, 329.
    Ligustrum lucidum compactum, 366.
    peach, 296.
    pecan, 324.
    plum, 316.
    raspberry, 321.
    Rosa sop., 373.
    Salix spp., 344.
  vesicatoria, pepper, 260.
    tomato, 277.
  viburni, Viburnum spp., 377.
  viridilivida, lettuce, 273.
  woodsii, Dianthus caryophyllus, 358.
Phytophthora sp., Citrus grandis, 300.
    Callistephus chinensis, 354.
    Lilium spp., 366.
    rhubarb, 286.
    strawberry, 208, 303.
    Syringa vulgaris, 375.
  cactorum, Antirrhinum majus, 351.
    apple, 308.
    Cornus spp., 339.
    Cornus florida, 357.
    Paeonia spp., 369.
    Rhododendron spp., 372.
    strawberry, 303.
    Syringa vulgaris, 375.
  capsici, pepper, 260.
  cryptogea richardiae, Zantedeschia
      sp., 377.
  erythroseptica, potato, 289.

Phytophthora infestans, potato, 190, 289.
  tomato, 277.
. megasperma, sweet clover, 240.
parasitica, Citrus spp., 300.
  tomato, 277.
. parasitica nicotianae, tobacco, 331.
phaseoli, lima bean, 280.
Pierce's disease (virus), grapevines, 323.
Piggotia fraxini, ash, 336.
Pink cherry (virus), sour cherry, 315.
Pink fruit, cherry, 315.
Piricularia grisea, Digitaria sanguinalis, 245.
  oryzae, rice, 229.
Pitya cupressi, Juniperus spp., 347.
Plant hosts, microorganisms and viruses in Hawaii, 3-36.
Plant pathogens and virus diseases, eastern Asia, host index, 93-123.
Plasmodiophora brassicae, Brassica oleracea var. broccoli, 255.
  cabbage, 258.
  cauliflower, 256.
  turnip, 259.
Plasmopara geranii, Geranium carolinianum, 361.
  viticola, grape, 209, 323.
Plenodomus destruens, sweetpotato, 272.
Pleospora lycopersici, tomato, 277.
Pod rot (undet.), peanut, 325.
Podosphaera spp., peach, 296.
  leucotricha, apple, 308.
  oxyacanthae, cherry, 314.
    sour cherry, 314.
    western chokecherry, 342.
    Wickson plum, 316.
Polyporus amarus, Libocedrus decurrens, 335.
  hirsutus, birch, 338.
  versicolor, Populus spp., 341.
  volvatus, Pinus contorta, 348.
Poor growth, Tsuga spp., 349.
Potash deficiency, cotton, 327.
  tobacco, 332.

Pratylenchus musicola, black walnut, 146.
  boxwood, 146.
  fig, 146.
  olive, 146.
  pratensis, Buxus sempervirens, 354.
  Chrysanthemum spp., 356.
  cotton, 146, 147.
  Gilia rubra, 362.
Proceedings, third national plant nematode conference, 135-150.
Pseudoperonospora cubensis, cantaloupe, 264.
  cucumber, 266.
  squash, 268.
  watermelon, 263.
  humuli, hops, 328, 329.
Pseudopeziza medicaginis, alfalfa, 239.
  ribis, currant, 319.
  gooseberry, 318.
  wild gooseberry, 318.
  trifolii, Trifolium pratense, 241.
Psyllid yellows (psyllids), potato, 191, 292.
  tomato, 278.
Puccinia spp., barley, 227.
  aemulans, Viguiera multiflora, 377.
  albulensis, Veronica wormskjoldii, 376.
  andropogonis, Andropogon furcatus, 244.
  Andropogon scoparius, 244.
  anomala, barley, 181, 227.
  antirrhini, Antirrhinum majus, 351.
  aristidae, Chenopodium rubrum, 355.
  Sarcobatus vermiculatus, 373.
  Triglochin maritima, 376.
  asparagi, asparagus, 252.
  atrofusca, Carex sp., 355.
  Carex deflexa, 355.
  balsamorhizae, Balsamorhiza sagittata, 353.
  bartholomaei, Bouteloua curtipendula, 244.
  bistortae, Polygonum viviparum, 371.
  canaliculata, Cyperus esculentus, 357.
  caricis, gooseberry, 318.
  caricis grossulariata, Ribes aureum, 319.
  Ribes setosum, 319.

Puccinia chrysanthemi, Chrysanthe-
    mum spp., 356.
  clintonii, Pedicularis paysoniana,
    369.
  convolvuli, Convolvulus arvensis,
    356.
  coronata, Calamagrostis rubescens,
    244.
    Elaeagnus canadensis, 359.
    Koeleria cristata, 245.
    oats, 185, 225.
    Rhamnus cathartica, 343.
  crandallii, Symphoricarpos albus,
    375.
    Symphoricarpos occidentalis,
    375.
  douglasii, Phlox glabrata, 370.
  extensicola, Carex festivella,
    355.
    Erigeron salsuginosus, 359.
  extensicola asteris, Aster sp.,
    352.
    Aster foliaceus var. apricus,
    352.
    Aster foliaceus var. canbyi,
    352.
  extensicola grossulariata,
    Agoseris glauca, 350.
  extensicola hieraciata, Hieracium
    scouleri, 363.
  fraxinata, Fraxinus spp., 340.
    green ash, 335.
  gayophyti, Gayophytum caesium, 361.
  glumarum, Elymus glaucus, 245.
    wheat, 231.
  graminis, Agrostis alba, 244.
    barley, 181, 227.
    oats, 184, 225.
    rye, 183, 230.
    wheat, 178, 179, 231.
  graminis phlei-pratensis, Phleum
    pratense, 246.
  grumosa, Zigadenus elegans, 378.
  harknessii, Stephanomeria pauci-
    flora, 374.
  helianthellae, Helianthella
    uniflora, 363.
  helianthi, Helianthus spp., 363.
    sunflower, 238.
  heterospora, Althaea rosea, 350.

Puccinia hieracii, Agoseris
    aurantiaca, 350.
    Pyrrhopappus carolinianus, 372.
    Taraxacum paludosum var. vulgare,
    375.
  iridis, Iris sp., 364
  jonesii, Lomatium sp., 366.
  leveillei, Geranium fremonti, 361.
  malvacearum, Althaea rosea, 350.
    Malva rotundifolia, 367.
  menthae, mint, 330.
    Monarda mollis, 367.
  monoica, Arabis sp., 352.
  obliqua, Gonolobus laevis, 362.
  obtegens, Cirsium arvense, 356.
  pimpinellae, Osmorhiza obtusa, 368.
  plumbaria, Phlox multiflora, 370.
  podophylli, Podophyllum peltatum, 371.
  purpurea, Sorghum halepense, 246.
  rubigo-vera, Aquilegia caerulea, 351
    Clematis ligusticifolia, 356.
    Ranunculus cymbalaria, 372.
    Ranunculus glaberrimus, 372.
  rubigo-vera agropyri, Thalictrum
    occidentale, 375.
  rubigo-vera apocrypta, Hydrophyllum
    capitatum, 364.
  rubigo-vera secalis, rye, 182, 230.
  rubigo-vera tritici, barley, 181, 22
    wheat, 178, 179, 232.
  smilacis, Smilax bona-nox, 374.
  solheimii, Dodecatheon pauciflorum,
    359.
  sorghi, field corn, 236.
    Sorghum vulgare sudanense, 246.
    sweet corn, 237.
  suksdorfii, Agoseris aurantiaca, 350
  tardissima, Arenaria congesta, 352.
  virgata, Sorghastrum nutans, 246.
  windsoriae, Ptelea trifoliata, 342.
    Triodia flava, 247.
  xanthii, Ambrosia trifida, 350.
    Xanthium sp., 377.
Pucciniastrum americanum, red rasp-
    berry, 321.
  goeppertianum, Abies lasiocarpa,
    346.
    huckleberry, 304.
    Vaccinium membranaceum, 376.
  myrtilli, Thuja canadensis, 349.

Pucciniastrum myrtilli, Vaccinium
    membranaceum, 376.
. pyrolae, Pyrola secunda, 372.
Purple top (virus), potato, 190.
Purple top wilt (undet.), potato, 293.
Pyrenopeziza medicaginis, alfalfa,
    239.
Pyrenophora teres, barley, 227.
Pythium sp., Agrostis spp., 243.
    Antirrhinum majus, 351.
    corn, 187, 236.
    cucumber, 267.
    flax, 228.
    garden beet, 253.
    lettuce, 273.
    pea, 283.
    pepper, 260.
    Phaseolus aureus, 280.
    Pinus spp.; 348.
    rhubarb, 286.
    sugar beet, 333.
    sugar cane, 334.
    tobacco, 330.
    tomato, 277.
    watermelon, 263.
    wheat, 231.
  acanthicum, watermelon, 263.
  aphanidermatum, potato, 290.
    radish, 286.
    sweetpotato, 272.
  arrhenomanes, sorghum, 230.
  butleri, field corn, 236.
  debaryanum, dasheen, 263.
    oats, 225.
    sugar beet, 333.
  debaryanum typo, pepper, 261.
  irregulare, spinach, 294.
  root rot, milo, see milo disease.
  ultimum, cowpea, 242.
    lettuce, 273.
    pea, 284.
    spinach, 294.
    sweetpotato, 189, 272.

              R

Ramularia sp., Leersia hexandra,
    245.
  armoraciae, horseradish, 285.
  asteris, Aster fremontii, 352.

Ramularia betae, sugar beet, 333.
  celtidis, Celtis occidentalis, 338.
· cynarae, globe artichoke, 270.
  heraclei, Heracleum lanatum, 363.
  pastinacae, parsnip, 280.
  primulae, Primula sp., 371.
  smilacinae, Smilacina racemosa, 374.
Ravenelia epiphylla, Tephrosia
    virginiana, 375.
Razoumofskya sp., Pseudotsuga taxifolia,
    348.
Red stele, strawberry, 208.
Red suture disease, peach, 298.
Rehmiellopsis bohemica, Abies concolor,
    346.
Rhabdocline pseudotsugae, Pseudotsuga
    taxifolia, 348.
Rhizoctonia sp., Azalea spp., 352.
    celery, 251.
    Chrysanthemum spp., 356.
    Dianthus caryophyllus, 358.
    Dolichos sphaerospermus, 359.
    Euphorbia spp., 360.
    garden beet, 253.
    Gardenia jasminoides, 361.
    Gladiolus spp., 362.
    pepper, 260.
    Pinus spp., 348.
    Stenotaphrum secundatum, 246.
    sugar beet, 333.
    tobacco, 330.
    undetermined Gramineae, 247.
  bataticola, Abutilon theophrasti,
      350.
    cotton, 325, 327.
    cowpea, 242.
    Erigeron canadensis, 359.
    Lactuca serriola, 365.
    Lespedeza stipulacea, 238.
    lima bean, 280.
    Phaseolus aureus, 280.
    soybean, 240.
    sweetpotato, 272.
    see also Sclerotium bataticola.
  microsclerotia, bean, 282.
  oryzae, rice, 229.
  solani, cotton, 325, 327.
    Cynodon dactylon, 244.
    Epidendrum sp., 359.
    garden beet, 253.

Rhizoctonia solani, Myrica spp., 367.
  pea, 284.
  Papaver orientale, 369.
  Pelargonium spp., 369.
  Petunia spp., 370.
  potato, 190.
  rhubarb, 286.
  rice, 229.
  sugar beet, 333.
  undetermined Gramineae, 247.
Rhizopus spp., cotton, 327.
  field corn, 235.
  prune, 313.
  squash, 268.
  sweetpotato, 189, 272.
  nigricans, peach, 296.
  strawberry, 303.
  sweetpotato, 272.
  rot, peach, 206.
Rhynchosporium secalis, barley, 223.
  rye, 230.
Rhytisma acerinum, Acer spp., 337.
  erythrosporum, Quercus
    virginiana, 343.
Ringspot (virus), Antirrhinum majus,
    351.
  apricot, 312.
  cabbage, 259.
  Dahlia spp., 357.
  tobacco, 332.
  tomato, 279.
Root diseases, strawberry, 208.
Root girdle (undet.), carrot, 270.
Root knot, peach, 206.
  tobacco, 202.
Root rot, dry beans, 197.
  field corn, 236.
  hops, 328.
  milo, see milo disease.
  Primula sp., 371.
  squash, 268.
  sugar beet, 200
Root and stem rots, green peas, 198,
    199.
Rosellinia necatrix, Osmanthus aqui-
    folium, 368.
Rosette (virus), peach, 299.
Rotylenchulus reniformis, cotton, 146.
  root parasite, 143.
Rugose mosaic (virus), potato, 292.
Running-out, carnation varieties, 359.

S

Salt injury (non-par.), celery, 252.
Savoy disease (virus), sugar beet, 334.
Scald (non-par.), apple, 310.
  onion, 250.
Scaly bark (virus ?), Citrus spp., 300.
Schizophyllum spp., ornamentals, 349.
Sclerospora macrospora, oats, 225.
Sclerotinia sp., Antirrhinum majus, 351
  cherry, 314.
  peach, 206, 297.
  Tulipa spp., 376.
  camelliae, Camellia japonica, 355.
  carunculoides, Morus alba, 311.
  convoluta, Iris sp., 364.
  fructicola, apple, 308.
  cherry, 207.
  peach, 206, 297.
  plum, 316.
  sour cherry, 314.
  sweet cherry, 314.
  gladioli, Gladiolus spp., 362.
  homoeocarpa, undetermined Gramineae,
    247.
  laxa, almond, 324.
  apricot, 312.
  cherry, 207.
  peach, 206.
  sclerotiorum, bean, 282.
  cabbage, 258.
  carrot, 270.
  cauliflower, 256.
  cucumber, 267.
  Helianthus spp., 363.
  lettuce, 273.
  Malvaviscus sp., 367.
  Matthiola incana, 367.
  Matthiola incana annua, 367.
  Paeonia spp., 369.
  pea, 285.
  potato, 290.
  squash, 268.
  strawberry, 303.
  winter squash, 269.
  trifoliorum, alfalfa, 239.
  clover, 241.
Sclerotium bataticola, corn, 187.
  field corn, 235.
  sorghum, 230.
  see also Rhizoctonia bataticola.

Sclerotium cepivorum, onion, 249.
    delphinii, Ageratum sp., 350.
        Antirrhinum majus, 351.
        Aquilegia spp., 351.
        Campanula medium, 355.
        Delphinium spp., 358.
        Eupatorium sp., 360.
        Trillium sp., 376.
        Viola spp., 377.
    oryzae, see Leptosphaeria
            salvinii.
    rolfsii, Allium sativum, 250.
        bean, 282.
        carrot, 270.
        Delphinium spp., 358.
        eggplant, 286.
        garden beet, 253.
        Hydrangea sp., 364.
        Iris sp., 364.
        Lespedeza stipulacea, 238.
        Lippia canescens, 366.
        peanut, 325.
        pepper, 261.
        potato, 290.
        sugar beet, 333.
        sugar cane, 334.
        tomato, 277.
Scolecotrichum graminis, Agrostis
            alba, 244.
        Phleum pratense, 246.
Scorias spongiosa, Fagus spp., 339.
Seed piece decay, potato, 293.
Seedling blights, cotton, 201, 327.
        rye, 183.
Septobasidium sydowii, Celtis
            occidentalis, 338.
Septoria sp., crabapple, 336.
        Fraxinus nigra, 340.
        hawthorn, 336.
        Panicum clandestinum, 246.
    apii, celery, 251.
    apii-graveolentis, celery, 251.
    azaleae, Azalea spp., 353.
    chrysanthemella, Chrysanthemum
            spp., 356.
    cucurbitacearum, squash, 268.
    gladioli, Gladiolus spp., 362.
    helianthi, Helianthus spp., 363.
    lactucae, lettuce, 273.
    lactucicola, Lactuca canadensis,
            365.

Septoria leaf spot, Chrysanthemum spp.,
        356.
    lycopersici, tomato, 192, 194, 277.
    nodorum, wheat, 233.
    obesa, Chrysanthemum sp., 356.
    philadelphi, Philadelphus spp., 370.
    phlogis, Phlox drummondii, 370.
    pisi, pea, 285.
    ribis, gooseberry, 319.
    rumicis, Rumex venosus, 373.
    signalensis, Symphoricarpos
            oreophilus, 375.
    symphoricarpi, Symphoricarpos spp.,
            375.
    tritici, wheat, 233
    veronicae, Veronica spp., 376.
Shoot rot, milo, see milo disease.
Silvering of foliage, peach, 299.
Skin breakdown, Florida oranges, 300.
Sooty mold, hops, 329.
Sorghum varieties and hybrids, reaction
            to milo disease, 165-175.
Sorosporium ellisii, Andropogon spp.,
            244.
    reilianum, popcorn, 237.
    syntherismae, Cenchrus pauciflorus,
            244.
Spanish measles (undet.), grape, 323.
Sphaceloma fawcettii, Citrus spp., 300.
    menthae, mint, 329.
    symphoricarpi, Symphoricarpos spp.,
            375.
    violae, Viola spp., 377.
Sphacelotheca cruenta, Sorghum hale-
            pense, 246.
    sorghi, sorghum, 230.
        Sorghum halepense, 246.
Sphaerella linorum, flax, 228.
Sphaeropsis sp., Juniperus virginiana,
            347.
        Nerium oleander, 368.
        Pinus spp., 348.
        Quercus spp., 343.
    ellisii, Pinus nigra austriaca, 348.
        Pinus sylvestris, 348.
    linearis, Carya sp., 338.
        Carya cordiformis, 338.
    ulmicola, Ulmus sp., 345.
Sphaerotheca castagnei, Taraxacum spp.,
            375.
    humuli, black raspberry, 321.

Sphaerotheca humuli, blackberry, 320.
 dewberry, 320.
 Geranium fremonti, 361.
 hops, 329.
 red raspberry, 321.
 strawberry, 303.
 Viola spp., 377.
 humuli fuliginea, Plantago eriopoda, 371.
 mors-uvae, currant, 319.
 gooseberry, 319.
 pannosa, peach, 297.
 Rosa spp., 373.
Spicaria spp., cotton, 327.
Spindle tuber (virus), potato, 292.
Spindling sprout, potato, 291.
Split pit (non-par.), peach, 299.
Spondylocladium atrovirens, potato, 291.
Sporidesmium scorzonerae, salsify, 294.
Sporocybe azaleae, Azalea spp., 353.
Spotted wilt (virus), celery, 252.
 Cosmos sulphureus, 357.
 lettuce, 274.
 pepper, 261.
 tomato, 195, 279.
 Zantedeschia sp., 377.
Spotting of berries (undet.), grape, 323.
Spray injury, apple, 311.
 cherry, 315.
 peach, 299.
 pear, 318.
Staghead, Ulmus spp., 345.
Stalk rots, corn, 186, 187.
 field corn, 235.
Stem cracking (non-par.), Euphorbia spp., 360.
Stemphylium sarcinaeforme, clover, 241.
 solani, tomato, 278.
Stereum purpureum, apple, 308.
 cherry, 314.
 rameale, birch, 338.
Stippen, apple, see bitter pit.
Stipple spot (undet.), peach, 299.
Stony pit (virus), pear, 318.
Storage rots, grapefruit, 301.

Storage rots, sweetpotato, 189.
Straighthead (non-par.); rice, 229.
Streak (virus), black raspberry, 322.
 green peas, 198.
 Rosa spp., 373.
 Senecio cruentus, 374.
 tobacco, 332.
 tomato, 195, 279.
Sulfur dioxide injury, grape, 323.
Sulfur fruit scald, apple, 311.
Sulfur leaf injury, apple, 311.
Summaries of tobacco diseases in 1939, 330.
Sunscald, apple, 311.
 asparagus, 253.
Sunscorch, fig, 301.
Synchytrium decipiens, Amphicarpa bracteata, 351.
 endobioticum, potato, 291.

T

Taphrina sp., sand cherry, 315.
 cerasi, cherry, 314.
 coerulescens, Quercus sp., 343.
  Quercus falcata f. triloba, 343.
  Quercus marilandica, 343.
  Quercus virginiana, 343.
 communis, plum, 316.
 crataegi, apple, 309.
 dearnessii, Acer spp., 337.
 deformans, peach, 206, 297.
 mirabilis, plum, 316.
 pruni, beach plum, 317.
 prune, 313.
 robinsoniana, Alnus incana, 337.
Thecaphora deformans, Astragalus bisulcatus, 352.
Thielaviopsis basicola, Lathyrus odoratus, 366.
 tobacco, 202, 331.
Tilletia spp., wheat, 173, 179.
 asperifolia, Muhlenbergia asperifolia, 367.
 horrida, rice, 229.
 levis, wheat, 233.
 tritici, wheat, 233.
Tip blight (non-par.), Antirrhinum majus, 351.
Tipburn (non-par.), cabbage, 259.

Tipburn, cauliflower, 256.
    lettuce, 273.
    potato, 191, 292.
Tobacco mosaic, pepper, 261.
Tranzschelia pruni-spinosae, plum,
    317.
    prune, 313.
    pruni-spinosae discolor, peach,
    298.
Trochila populorum, Populus spp.,
    341.
Tubercularia fici, fig, 301.
Typhula sp., undetermined Gramineae,
    247.

U

Uncinula sp., Parthenocissus
    quinquefolia, 369.
    necator, grape, 209, 323.
    salicis, Salix sp., 344.
        Salix glaucophylla var., 344.
Urocystis cepulae, onion, 249.
    occulta, rye, 182, 230.
Uromyces betae, sugar beet, 333.
    caladii, Arisaema dracontium,
        352.
    caryophyllinus, Dianthus caryo-
        phyllus, 358.
    coloradensis, vetch, 242.
    elegans, Trifolium carolinianum,
        241.
        Trifolium procumbens, 241.
    graminicola, Panicum virgatum,
        246.
        Stillingia sylvatica, 374.
    hedysari-obscuri, Hedysarum
        marginatum, 363.
    heterodermus, Erythronium
        grandiflorum, 360.
    intricatus, Eriogonum
        campanulatum, 360.
    jonesii, Ranunculus calthae-
        florus, 372.
    lapponicus, Oxytropis gracilis,
        368.
    lespedezae-procumbentis,
        Lespedeza spp., 238.
    minor, Trifolium parryi, 241.
    peckianus, Plantago aristata,
        371.

Uromyces peckianus, Plantago purshii,
    371.
    phaseoli typica, bean, 283.
    green beans, 196.
    lima bean, 280.
    phaseoli vignae, cowpea, 243.
    shearianus, Atriplex corrugata,
        352.
    spermacoces, Diodia teres, 359.
    striatus, alfalfa, 239.
    trifolii, clover, 241.
    trifolii fallens, clover, 241.
        Trifolium pratense, 241.
    trifolii hybridi, Trifolium
        hybridum, 242.
    trifolii trifolii-repentis,
        Trifolium repens, 242.
    zygadeni, Zigadenus gramineus, 378.
Ustilago spp., barley, 228.
    Bromus spp., 244.
    avenae, oats, 184, 226.
    bromivora, Bromus spp., 244.
    crusgalli, Echinochloa crusgalli,
        245.
    cynodontis, Cynodon dactylon, 245.
    hordei, barley, 180, 228.
        rye, 230.
    hypodytes, Agropyron spp., 243.
    levis, oats, 184, 226.
    lorentziana, Hordeum jubatum, 245.
    nigra, barley, 228.
    nuda, barley, 180, 228.
    rabenhorstiana, Digitaria sanguin-
        alis, 245.
    striaeformis, Agrostis alba, 244.
        Phleum pratense, 246.
    tritici, wheat, 178, 179, 233.
    zeae, corn, 186, 187.
        field corn, 236.
        sweet corn, 188, 237.

V

Valsa spp., peach, 298.
    Populus sp., 342.
    celtidis, Celtis occidentalis, 338.
    cincta, peach, 298.
    leucostoma, peach, 298.
Venturia sp., Pyracantha sp., 372.
    inaequalis, apple, 204, 205, 309.

Venturia inaequalis orbicularis,
    Crataegus sop., 339.
  pyrina, pear, 203, 318.
Vermicularia sp., Carya spp., 338.
    Ulmus spp., 345.
Verticillium sp., Acer platanoides,
    337.
    Acer pseudo-platanus, 337.
    Acer saccharum, 337.
    Antirrhinum majus, 351.
    Aucuba sp., 352.
    Berberis thunbergii, 353.
    blackberry, 320.
    Chrysanthemum morifolium, 356.
    eggplant, 286.
    Phlox paniculata, 370.
    raspberry, 322.
    Rhus aromatica, 343.
    strawberry, 303.
    sugar beet, 334.
    tomato, 273.
    Ulmus spp., 345.
    Ulmus americana, 345.
    Viburnum tinus, 377.
  albo-atrum, Acer spp., 337.
    Antirrhinum majus, 351.
    apricot, 312.
    black raspberry, 321.
    Boysenberry, 320.
    Brassica oleracea var. napo-
        brassica, 254.
    Chrysanthemum spp., 356.
    cotton, 327.
    Dahlia spp., 357.
    eggplant, 286.
    okra, 271.
    Paeonia spp., 369.
    peach, 298.
    pepper, 261.
    Phlox spp., 370.
    purple raspberry, 322.
    red raspberry, 322.
    Rhus spp., 343.
    sweetpotato, 272.
    tomato, 193, 195, 278.
    youngberry, 322.
  dahliae, Senecio cruentus, 374.
Virus diseases, bean, 233.
    cabbage, 259.
    celery, 252.

Virus diseases, cherry, 315.
    cucumber, 267.
    dry beans, 197.
    garden beet, 253.
    green beans, 196.
    green peas, 198, 199.
    hops, 328, 329.
    lettuce, 273.
    peach, 206, 298.
    pepper, 261.
    potato, 190, 291.
    raspberry, 322.
    strawberry, 304.
    sugar beet, 334.
    tobacco, 332.
    tomato, 193, 195, 278.
Virus diseases and plant pathogens,
    eastern Asia, host index,
    93-123.
Viruses, in Hawaii and their hosts, 82-
    84.

W

Wart (undet.), peach, 299.
Wasting disease, Zostera marina, 378.
Water core (non-par.), apple, 311.
Weak hills, hops, 329.
Weather injury, Abies spp., 346.
    apple, 311.
    cherry, 315.
    Delphinium spp., 358.
    Kalmia latifolia, 365.
    peach, 300.
    pear, 318.
    prune, 313.
    Rhododendron spp., 372.
    strawberry, 304.
    Taxus spp., 349.
    wheat, 233.
Western celery mosaic (virus), celery,
    252.
Western yellow mosaic (virus), celery,
    252.
White mottling of leaves (virus),
    Jatropha stimulosa, 365.
White streak (virus), Narcissus sp.,
    367.
White tip (non-par.), rice, 229.
Wind injury, apple, 311.

Wind injury, lettuce, 274.
Wind and sand injury, tomato, 278.
Winter injury, Abies spp., 346.
    alfalfa, 240.
    apple, 311.
    black raspberry, 322.
    grape, 323.
    Juniperus spp., 347.
    peach, 300.
    purple raspberry, 322.
    red raspberry, 322.
    strawberry, 304.
    sweet cherry, 316.
    Taxus spp., 349.
    wheat, 233.
Witches' broom, alfalfa, 240.
    clover, 242.
    strawberry, 304.
    western yew, 349.

X

Xylaria mali, apple, 310.

Y

Yellow dwarf (virus), onion, 250.

Yellow dwarf (virus), potato, 292.
Yellow mosaic (virus), bean, 283.
    sugar cane, 324.
Yellow-red virosis (virus), chokecherry, 299.
    peach, 299.
    Prunus virginiana, 315, 342.
    Prunus virginiana var. demissa, 315.
Yellow spotting of leaves (undet.), peach, 299.
Yellow vein (undet.), peach, 299.
Yellowing and stunting (non-par.) Delphinium spp., 358.
Yellows (undet.), Sassafras albicum, 344.
Yellows (virus), Callistephus chinensis, 354.
    carrot, 270.
    Cichorium endivia, 261.
    Dianthus caryophyllus, 359.
    peach, 299.
    strawberry, 304.
    tomato, 278.
Yellow top, tomato, 279.

Z

Z-disease, potato, see Fusarium solani eumartii.

ERRATA

On page 254 under Brassica campestris, read Erysiphe polygoni instead of Erysiphe graminis.

On page 278, 2d paragraph from bottom read psyllid instead of pyllid.

On page 283, last paragraph read Aphanomyces euteiches instead of Alphanomyces euteiches.

On page 298 last paragraph delete under phony peach "and in Oklahoma a trace loss." Phony peach was not reported from Oklahoma in 1939.

On page 340 under Fraxinus spp., read Cylindrosporium sp. instead of Clylindrosporium.

On page 351 under Antirrhinum majus, Sclerotinia sp., "S. delphinii" should be read Sclerotium delphinii, not Sclerotinia.

CPSIA information can be obtained
at www.ICGtesting.com
Printed in the USA
LVHW021510261118
598291LV00012B/1197